The Beginner's Guide to

# SAMSUNG

## GALAXY S20 SERIES

The Complete Guide to Mastering Your
Samsung Galaxy S20, S20 Plus and S20 Ultra

**THOMAS JACKSON**

# Copyright

# Table of Content

## Why This Guide

So, you just got your Samsung Galaxy S20, S20 plus and S20 Ultra, that's great! Now that you are here, we have detailed instructions you need to guide you through setting it up for the first time.

The Guides in this book are essentials for iPhone switchers or novice Android users who wish to navigate the Galaxy S20, S20 plus and S20 Ultra with ease.

## About the Author

Thomas Jackson is a tech enthusiast with about 10 years' experience in the ICT industry. He is passionate about the latest technical and technological trends. Thomas holds a Bachelor and a master's degree in Computer Science and Information Communication Technology respectively from MIT, Boston Massachusetts.

# Getting Started

## What's inside the box

Contained in the box are;

- ➤ The phone (Galaxy S20/S20+/S20 Ultra).

- ➤ 45-watt power brick

- ➤ An ejector pin for ejecting the SIM tray

- ➤ A USB-C charge cable.

- ➤ A pair of wired AKG earbuds that do connect to the USB -C port

# The Hardware

## Galaxy S20

Flash

Rear cameras

Front camera

Volume keys

Side key

Fingerprint scanner

USB charger/Audio port

# Galaxy S20+

Front camera

Flash

Volume keys

Side key

Rear cameras

Fingerprint
scanner

USB charger/Audio port

# Galaxy S20 Ultra

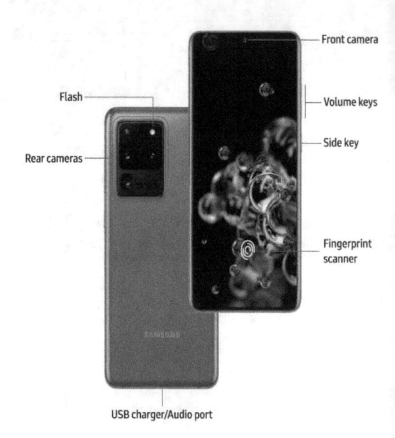

Front camera

Flash

Volume keys

Side key

Rear cameras

Fingerprint
scanner

USB charger/Audio port

## Insert the SIM Card

- Insert the ejection pin into the hole on the tray to loosen the tray.
- The SIM card try has an expandable slot that supports up to 512GB of MicroSD storage.

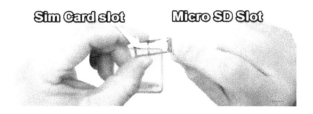

- Place the SIM card on the SIM card slot with the gold-colored contacts facing downwards.

## Initial Setup

Press and hold the power button to power the device for the first time. We have "Let's go!", "English", "Emergency call" and "Accessibility" on the setup wizard screen.

- Select your preferred English option and click on the forward arrow icon. At the background of the setup screen, you will hear some voice prompts giving you instructions on how to setup the device.

- The next screen displays the Terms and Conditions for using the device. "End User License Agreement", "diagnostic data", "information linking" and "marketing information" are displayed. Tap on "End User License Agreement".

- Tap "Next" to proceed.

- On this screen, you are prompted to "Bring your old data for quicker setup". This will retrieve your data from a previous smartphone to the new Galaxy S20. You can transfer the data wirelessly or by using Cable and USB connector.

Bring your old data
for quicker setup

Bring your settings, contacts, apps, photos,
music, and more from your previous device.
Terms of Service. Permissions

How do you want to connect?

○  Wireless
   Only available with Samsung Galaxy devices

○  Cable and USB connector
   iPhone, Android, etc.

○  Skip this for now

<   Next

- If you wish to retrieve settings from another smartphone e.g. a Samsung Galaxy S9 or an iPhone – tap on the Cable and USB connector and tap on "Next".

- Tap on the "Skip this for now" then tap "Next" if you wish to retrieve data from an old smartphone after setup is complete.

- The next step is to set up a Wi-Fi connection. Choose a Wi-Fi or add a network manually by clicking the "Add Network" button. Select your Wi-Fi network if it is available and key in the password; tap on "Connect". Enable the "Auto

8

reconnect" to automatically connect to your Wi-Fi network without having to enter a password every time you wish to reconnect to your Wi-Fi network. Move to the next setup page by tapping "Next".

- The phone checks for updates to make sure the device is operating on the latest software.
- Log into your google account and click "Next". If you have a Google backup available, you will

be prompted to "choose a backup to restore" else tap on "Don't restore".

- Next is to setup Privacy security. You are requested to protect your personal information by preventing others from accessing your device by activating device protection features such as "Face recognition", "Fingerprints", "Pattern", "PIN" or "Password". If you wish to skip this process click on "Not Now". Tap on "Fingerprints" to setup the fingerprints, a page displays with tips on using fingerprints, click on "Continue". You will need to setup PIN backup in case you have difficulties unlocking the device with your fingerprints. Click on "PIN" and enter a passcode, key in the passcode for a second time to confirm it, then click on "OK". The next process requests you to place your finger on the sensor, then lift it off when you feel a vibration. You will be requested to press a little harder or to rotate your finger slightly each

10

time to cover the entire index fingerprint. The device will ask you to scan the edges of your fingers to get a full scan. You can add more fingerprints by clicking on "Add".

- Click on "Next"
- Click on "Accept" to agree to Google services terms and conditions.
- If the recommended apps screen appears, select the apps you want and download them.
- Sign-in to your Samsung Account and click "Next." You get the All done message which indicates that you are good to go. Tap "Finish" to complete the initial setup. The Galaxy S20 Home Screen.
- Click on "Update" when this request pops up.

## Transferring Data from Your Previous Device

You can connect your previous device to your device with the USB connector (USB-C) and a USB cable to easily and quickly transfer data.

- The first step is to connect the other device to your Galaxy S20 with the aid of a USB Type-C cable. Plug the USB adapter (USB-C) into the multipurpose jack of your phone.

- After the connection is made, a notification pops up at the bottom of the S20 screen. If this notification does not pop up, unplug the USB-C cable and plug it back again.

- The notification pop-up requires you to choose an app for the USB device to take action on.

- Here, we are going to tap on "Smart Search" because that's the app that will transfer everything from the old phone to the new phone, then select "Just once".

- A dialogue box pops-up next asking if you want to send or receive data. Tap on "Receive data."

- Then on the old phone, you will receive a notification asking you to "Allow access to phone data?" Click on "Allow."

- Now the Galaxy S20 would scan through the old phone to find the different contents that can be transferred. This will take about a minute and it will allow you to choose what item(s) you wish to transfer. It displays the number of items that can be transferred (for example – call and contacts, messages, applications (excluding the app data), settings, home screen settings, videos, images, documents, audio), their sizes and total time it would take to transfer them are displayed. If you don't want a particular item(s) to be transferred, all you have to do is just unselect the particular item(s). To show items that cannot be transferred, tap on "Find out what we can't bring." Items that can't be transferred include calls and contacts that are Read Only, Emergency Alert messages, some information from apps like Calendar events that are sync through Google accounts, some apps can't be transferred due to security compatibility (e.g. Samsung Pay information), movie makers, Galaxy wearable apps, default wallpapers etc.

- After selecting the apps, you wish to transfer to your Galaxy S20, tap on "Transfer." A pop-up screen comes up telling you how long it is going to take and on what percentage the transfer is at. During the transfer, you would see what it is working on in the middle of the device. When the transfer process is complete, a notification pops up on the screen telling you to disconnect the cable. The pages of the items transferred would be displayed and the apps that could not be transferred will also be displayed.

## Wireless PowerShare

Wireless PowerShare is a cool feature where the Galaxy S20 can wirelessly charge other devices. This feature was designed mainly to enable the S20 to charge accessories like the Galaxy watch and Galaxy Buds. To use this feature:

- Swipe down from the top of the screen.
- Swipe down for a second time to reveal the full set of quick toggles.
- Tap on "Wireless PowerShare.
- Follow the instructions displayed on the screen.

When making use of Wireless PowerShare to charge another phone, check that both devices are placed with their backs to each other. For Galaxy buds, just place the case back of the S20 and it will start charging.

When you're done charging, remove the device that is being charged and tap Cancel at the bottom of the Galaxy S20's screen to turn Wireless Power Share off.

# Home Screen Settings

## Fixing Device Redundancy

To fix redundancies, pinch on the screen to reveal the Home Screen Settings.

- Click the "Home Screen Settings
- Enable the swipe down for notification panel.

Now when you go to the Home Screen and swipe from top down, it actually brings down the notification panel, when you swipe further down, the notification panel expands giving you access to quick toggles. When you swipe from bottom-up, it displays the App drawer.

## Disable Apps Button

You can disable the Apps button at the lower right corner of your device screen in case it is enabled. To do this,

- Pinch on the Home screen
- Tap on "Home Screen Settings"

- Disable the "Apps button" toggle if it is enabled

Now that the App button gone from the App Dock, you will now have one more extra room for an extra App.

## Wallpaper

You can change how the Home and Lock screens by choosing a favorite picture, video, or preloaded wallpaper. To do this;

- Pinch on the Home Screen
- Tap on wallpapers
- Click one of the following menus for available wallpapers:
  - My wallpapers: Choose from featured and downloaded wallpapers.
  - Gallery: Choose pictures and videos saved on your device

- Wallpaper services: Enable additional features including guide page and Dynamic Lock screen.
- Apply Dark mode to Wallpaper: Enable to apply Dark mode to your wallpaper.
- Explore more wallpapers: Download wallpapers from Galaxy Themes.
- Click on a picture or video to select it.
  - If you are selecting a single picture, choose which screen or screens you wish to apply the wallpaper to.
  - You can only apply Videos and multiple pictures to the Lock screen.
- Depending on the applicable screen, click on "Set on Home screen", "Set on Lock screen", or "Set on Home and Lock screens".

# Multipack Wallpaper Option

This option when enabled allows you to see different wall papers each time the device screen is locked. To achieve this effect,

- Pinch on the Home Screen
- Tap on wallpapers
- Tap on "View All" and make sure you choose the multipack option. When you pick the multipack option, the just has the ability to choose random wallpaper from a list of wallpapers that you have downloaded.

## Placing Apps in a Folder

Several apps on the Home Screen can be placed in a folder. All you have to do is press and hold one of the Apps you want in a folder until options pop up –tap on "select items," then select the apps you wish to group together and then click on "Create folder" at the top right corner of the Home screen and a folder is created. You can give the folder a name and pick a color for the folder.

To undo the folder, click on it – press and hold one of the app icons in the folder, tap on "select items" from the option pop up to select all the apps in the folder – tap on each app to select and group them, then drag them out to the Home screen.

## Easy mode

The Easy mode layout has larger text and icons, making for a more straightforward visual experience. Switch between the default screen layout and a simpler layout.

- From Settings, tap on Display > Easy mode.

- Click on the toggle to enable this feature. The following options appear:

  - Touch and hold delay: Set how long it takes for a continuous touch to be recognized as a touch and hold.

  - High contrast keyboard: Choose a keyboard with high contrast colors.

## Notification panel

For quick access to notifications, settings, and more, simply open the Notification panel.

You can access the Notification panel from any screen.

- Drag the Status bar down to display the Notification panel.

- Swipe down the list to see notification details.

  - To open an item, tap it.

    - To clear a single notification, drag the notification left or right.

21

- To clear all notifications, tap Clear.

- To customize notifications, tap Notification settings.

- Drag upward from the bottom of the screen or click on Back to close the Notification panel.

## Accounts & Security

Set up and manage your accounts. If you skipped the Security and Privacy settings during the initial set up process for your device, this can be done after the phone has been set up. Use biometrics to securely unlock your device and log in to accounts.

## Add a Google Account

Sign in to your Google Account to access your Google Cloud Storage, apps installed from your account, and make full use of your device's Android™ features.

- From Settings, tap 🔑 Accounts and backup, click on Accounts.

- Tap ✚ Add account, then tap Google.

## Add a Samsung account

Sign-in to your Samsung account to access exclusive Samsung content and make full use of Samsung apps.

- From Settings, tap 🔑 Accounts and backup > Accounts.

- Tap ✚ Add account > Samsung account.

## Face recognition

You can enable Face Recognition to unlock your screen. To use your face to unlock your device, you must set a pattern, PIN, or password.

- Face recognition is less secure than Pattern, PIN, or Password. Your device could be unlocked by someone or something that looks like your image.

- Some conditions may affect face recognition, including wearing glasses, hats, beards, or heavy make-up.

- When registering your face, ensure that you are in a well-lit area and the camera lens is clean.

  1. From Settings, click on Biometrics and security, then tap on Face recognition.

24

2. Follow the prompts to register your face.

## Face recognition management

You can customize how you want the face recognition feature to work. To do this;

- Go to Settings, click on Biometrics and security
- Tap Face recognition. You will get the following options:
  - Remove face data: Delete existing faces.
  - Add alternative look: Enhance face recognition by adding an alternative appearance.
  - Face unlock: Enable or disable face recognition security.
  - Stay on Lock screen: When you unlock your device with face recognition, stay on the Lock screen until you swipe the screen.
  - Faster recognition: Turn on for faster face recognition. You should be aware that

enabling this option makes it easy to unlock the device using an image or video of your likeness.

o Require open eyes: Performs facial recognition only when they eyes are open.

o Brighten screen: Temporarily increases the screen brightness so that your face can be recognized in dark conditions.

o Samsung Pass: Access your online accounts using face recognition.

## Fingerprint Scanner

Fingerprint recognition can be used as an alternative to entering passwords in certain apps. To use your fingerprint to unlock your device, you must set a pattern, PIN, or password. To do this;

- Go to Settings
- Click on Biometrics and security, then tap Fingerprints.

- Follow the instructions to register your fingerprint.

## Fingerprint Management

To Add, delete, and rename fingerprints.

- Go to Settings
- Click on Biometrics and security, then tap Fingerprints. The following options are:
  - The list of registered fingerprints is at the top of this list. You can tap a fingerprint to delete or rename it.
  - Add fingerprint: Follow the instructions to add another fingerprint.
  - Check added fingerprints: Scan your fingerprint to see if it has been added.
  - Fingerprint unlock: Use your fingerprint when unlocking your device.
  - Show icon when screen is off: Show the fingerprint icon when the screen is off.

o Samsung Pass: Use your fingerprint for identification when using supported apps.

o Samsung Pay: Use your fingerprints to make payments quickly and securely.

## Setup the Secure Folder for the First Time

- Go to settings

- Scroll down and tap on "Biometrics and security."

- Scroll down "Secure folder" and tap on it.

- Click on "Continue"

- You will be prompted to enter your Samsung account password, key your password and press ok.

- Pick a unique Pattern, PIN or Password for the Secure folder, it does not have to be the same PIN or Password you use to unlock your phone. Also make sure the Fingerprints toggle is enabled. Click on next

- Key in your PIN, Password or Pattern depending on the option you selected.
- Now click on the ellipse at the top right corner to reveal some options, click on "Settings"
- Tap on "Auto lock Secure Folder"
- Select "Immediately"

## How to hide photos

- Go to gallery
- Tap on the picture
- Tap on the ellipse on the top right corner to reveal options
- Tap on "Move to secure Folder"
- Enter your PIN or scan your Finger

## Hide Multiple Photos

- Go to gallery
- Press and hold to select the pictures
- Tap on the ellipse on the top right corner to reveal options
- Tap on "Move to secure Folder"

- Enter your PIN or scan your Fingerprint

# Connection Settings

Manage connections between your device and a variety of networks and other devices.

## Connect to Wi-Fi

Connect your device to a Wi-Fi network to access the Internet without making use of your mobile data. To do this;

- Go to settings
- Tap 🛜Connections > Wi-Fi
- Tap on the toggle to turn on Wi-Fi and scan for networks that are available.
- Click on a network, key in password if required.

## Pair Bluetooth Device

You can pair your device to other Bluetooth-enabled devices, like Bluetooth headphones. To pair a Bluetooth device;

- Go to Settings, click on Connections > Bluetooth, and tap on the toggle to turn on Wi-Fi

- Click on the device you which to pair and follow the prompts to connect.

## Mobile hotspot

Mobile hotspot uses your data plan to create a Wi-Fi network that can be used by multiple devices.

You can customize your mobile hotspot's security and connection settings.

- Go to Settings
- Click on Connections > Mobile hotspot and tethering > Mobile hotspot.
- Tap on More options, click on "Configure mobile hotspot" for the following settings:
  - Network name: View and rename of your Mobile hotspot.
  - Hide my device: Prevent other devices from discovering your Mobile hotspot.

32

- Security: Select the security level for your Mobile hotspot.

- Password: View or change your hotspot password.

- Power saving mode: Reduce battery usage by analyzing hotspot traffic.

- Protected management frames: Enable this feature for additional privacy protections.

To turn on mobile hotspot;

- Go to Settings
- Click on Connections > Mobile hotspot and tethering > Mobile hotspot.
- Tap the toggle to turn on Mobile hotspot.

To change mobile hotspot password

- Go to Settings
- Click on Connections > Mobile hotspot and tethering > Mobile hotspot.

- Click the password box, key in a new password, and then tap Save.

## Navigation bar

You may navigate your device by using either the navigation buttons or full screen gestures.

You can use either the full-screen gestures or the navigation bar buttons on the Galaxy S20.

- Go to "Settings"
- Tap on "Display"
- Click on "Navigation bar"

The navigation buttons at the bottom of the Screen will be eliminated if "Full screen gestures" is enabled. In the absence of the navigation buttons, only swipe movements can be used to navigate through your device.

Using the full screen gestures, you can go to the Home Screen if you swipe from center up, to go one step backwards, swipe up from the bottom right corner and swipe up from the bottom left corner to view all your recent apps.

When on "Full Screen Gestures", you can eliminate the line at the bottom of the screen to enjoy full screen experience by disabling the "Gesture Hints."

When using the "navigation buttons", the positions of the buttons can be switched by selecting the "button order" of your choice.

**Button order**   ·················································

  ◉          III        O         &lt;

  ○          &lt;        O        III

## Edge Lighting

Edge Lighting is a fun way to view and interact with your notifications. When Edge Lighting is enabled, notifications will be replaced by the edge of the screen lighting up. To enable the edge lighting

- Swipe down the notification panel
- Tap the "Settings" icon
- Click on "Display"
- Under "Display" scroll down and click on "Edge Screen".
- Edge screen is the area of your settings where you can make changes to your Edge panels and change the settings for your edge lighting. When Edge Lighting is enabled, the prominent banner that usually pops up when a text message is received is replayed by a smaller icon.

- Edge Lighting displays in different ways, tap "Show Edge Lighting" and you will be able to set it up to always show Edge Lighting when the screen is ON or it will only show it when the screen is OFF. You can also set Edge Lighting to Always whether the screen is ON or OFF.

SHOW EDGE LIGHTING

○  When screen is on

○  When screen is off

◉  Always

- "Edge Lighting Style" is where you can change your edge lighting effects. Underneath "Effect" you have the option for bubble, multicolor, Glow effect and Glitter. There are ways you can edit the "Effect."

- Click on "Effect"

- Click on the effect you wish to use

- To choose a color of the effect, click on "Color"

- Select the color you wish to use

- Tap "Done" when you have made all your changes

- You can also interact with notification using "Edge lighting interaction." When this feature is enabled, you would be able to do several things with the little icon that pops up at the top of the screen. You can the app in pop-up view by double tapping on the pop up, a small pop-up window is opened if you swipe down on the pop-up icon, to dismiss the edge lighting notification, simply swipe-left or swipe-right on the pop up.

## Making calls

- From the Home screen, tap on the phone icon and then tap on the keypad

- Enter a number on the keypad and tap 🔵 to make a Call.

+ Add to Contacts

(817) 555-1510

| 1 | 2 | 3 |
|---|---|---|
| 4 | 5 | 6 |
| 7 | 8 | 9 |
| * | 0 | # |

## Enable swipe to call

Swipe a contact or number to the right to make a call. To enable this feature;

- Go to Settings
- Click on Advanced features, then on Motions and gestures, tap on Swipe to call or send messages.
- Tap on the toggle to enable this feature.

## Call pop-up settings

- When calls are received while using other apps, they can be displayed as pop-ups.
- Launch the phone app, tap on the ⋮ top right corner of the screen
- Tap on Settings, then tap Call display while using apps. The following options are available:
  - Full screen: Display an incoming call in the full screen Phone app.
  - Pop-up: Display an incoming call as a pop-up at the top of the screen.

43

- Mini pop-up: Display an incoming call as a smaller pop-up.
- Keep calls in pop-up: Enable this option to keep calls in the pop-up after they are answered.

## How to enable Caller ID and spam protection

- Launch the dialer from the home screen.
- Click on the overflow menu (three vertical dots on the right), then tap on Settings.

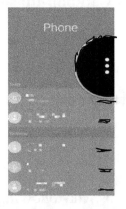

- Tap the Caller ID and spam protection toggle to enable it.
- Read Hiya's privacy policy and select the boxes.
- Tap Agree to finish.

## How to enable Wi-Fi Calling

- Go to Settings

- Click on Connections.

- Tap the Wi-Fi Calling toggle to enable.

## How to use Google Duo

- Go to the phone dialer.

- Select the contact you want to video call.

- Click on the Duo icon underneath the contact's details to initiate a video call.

- The video call will be transferred over to Duo.

- You can switch from a regular voice call to a video call. When you're on a call, hit the Video call button to switch to Duo.

# How to Store Contacts

Store and manage your contacts. You can synchronize with personal accounts added to your device. Accounts may also support email, calendars, and other features.

- Go to Apps, click on the contact icon. Doing so brings up the list of existing contacts

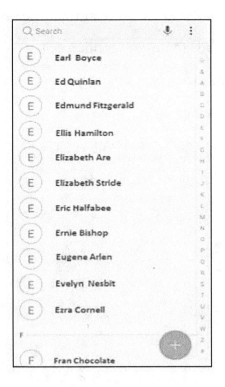

- Tap on the create contact icon.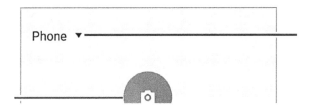

Select the contact to storage location

- When you tap on, it displays other storage options in a drop down.

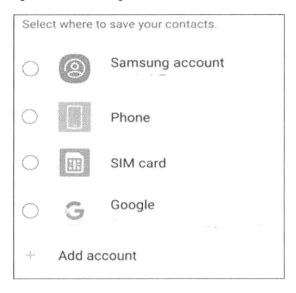

- Enter contact information and click on Save.

Alternatively, you can add a contact directly from the Call app. To do this;

- From the Home screen, tap on the phone icon and then tap on the keypad
- Enter a number on the keypad, then tap Add to Contacts.

- Follow the same procedure as the previous method.

## Edit a contact

When updating a contact, you can tap a field and change or delete information, or you can add more fields to the contact's list of information.

- Launch the Contact App, then click on a contact.

- Click on Edit.

- Tap any of the fields to add, change, or delete information.

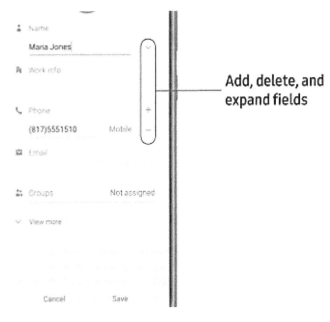

Add, delete, and expand fields

- Tap Save.

# Customization

## Rename Your Phone

- Go to settings
- Tap on "About Phone"
- Tap on "Edit" to rename phone
- This setting displays the custom name you gave to your phone when connecting to other devices via Bluetooth making your device easily recognizable.

## Side Key Settings

The side key is a Bixby/power button. When you press it once, the screen goes off and when you press gain the screen comes on. You do have the option to customize this.

- Go to settings
- Scroll down and tap on Advance features
- On the Advance features menu, click on side key

From the displayed page, you can customize the "Double press" and the "Press and hold" options.

- Under the Press and hold heading, tap an option:
  - Wake Bixby (default)
  - Power off menu
- Tap Double press to enable this feature, and tap an option:
  - Quick launch camera (default)
  - Open Bixby
  - Open app

## Taking Calls with Volume Button and Ending Calls with Side Key

- Tap on the phone call application
- Tap on the Ellipses at the top right corner to reveal the "Settings"- Click on "Settings."
- In the call settings, tap on "Answering and Ending Calls"

- Tap on the toggle switch to enable "Press volume up to answer."
- If you want to end calls with the Side key, just tap on the toggle switch to enable "Press Side key to end."

## Enable 120Hz

To enable the 120Hz refresh rate, your device screen resolution as to be set at FHD+. To do this;

- Go to settings
- Tap on display
- Click on screen resolution and change to FHD+, tap on apply.

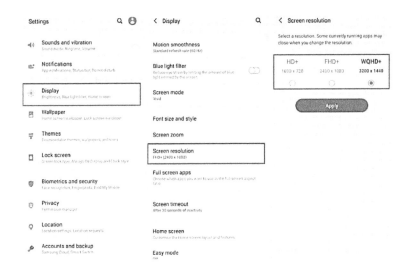

To enable the high refresh rate,

- Go to settings
- Click on display
- Tap on motion smoothness
- Click on High refresh rate to select 120Hz
- Tap Apply

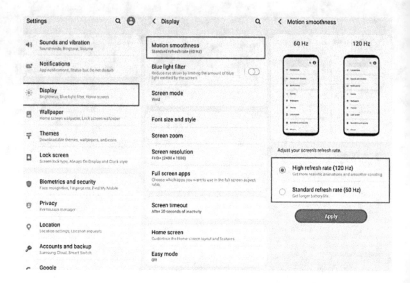

## Show Battery Percentage Meter

By default, the battery icon at the top of the home screen of your device does not display a percentage meter. The percentage meter shows you how much battery is remaining. To replace the battery icon with the percentage of your battery,

- Go to "Settings"
- Tap on "Notifications"
- Click "Status bar"
- Toggle on "Show battery percentage"

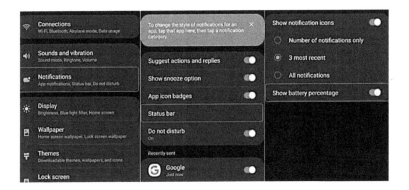

## Dark Mode

Dark mode allows you to change how your device looks on the Screen. When night mode is enabled, you have a black background and white text. This background also affects the entire Samsung core Apps on the phone. Night mode can be activated by:

- Going to "settings"
- Tap "Display"
- Tap "Dark" to enable it.

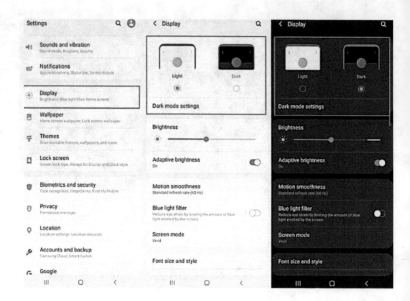

You can also set schedules for when you want to use Dark mode.

To do this Tap on "Dark mode settings", there are two options you can choose from; "Turn on now" and "Turn on as scheduled".

Under "Turn on as scheduled" you can either choose "Sunset to sunrise" or "Custom schedule".

Apply to wallpaper: Apply Dark mode settings to the wallpaper when it is active.

Adaptive color filter: Turn on Blue light filter automatically between sunset and sunrise to reduce eye strain.

## Screen brightness

You can adjust the screen brightness according to lighting conditions or personal preference. To do this:

- Go to Settings, click Display.
- Customize the options under Brightness:
    - Drag the Brightness slider left or right to set a custom brightness level.
    - Click on Adaptive brightness to automatically adjust the screen brightness based on the lighting conditions.

## Font size and style

You can customize your device by changing the font size and style. To do this;

- Go to Settings, click on Display, then click on Font size and style. The following options appear:
  - Click on Font style to choose a different font. Click on a font to select it, or click Download fonts to add fonts from Galaxy Store.
  - Tap Bold font to make all fonts appear with bold weight.
  - Drag the Font size slider to adjust the text size.

## Multitasking Split Screen

To split your device screen for multitasking-

- Hold down on the "Recent Apps" button. For it to work do ensure that you have some recent apps opened.

- Hold down the app icon to pop up several options – "App info", "change app aspect ratio", "Lock this app", "Open in split screen view" and "Pin this App."

- Click on "Open in split screen view." The split screen can be adjusted by holding down on the borderline and moving it either up or down.

## Always On Display

View missed calls and message alerts, check the time and date, and view other customized information without unlocking your device using Always On Display (AOD).

- Click on settings from the home screen or the app drawer.
- Navigate down and tap on "Lock screen".
- Toggle Always on display to enable it.
- Click on Always On Display, then select the options that you prefer.

It should be noted that the show always options consumes battery life more.

## How to customize Always On Display

There are a lot of ways to customize your experience with Always On Display. You can choose to schedule to disable it at night, show up all the time. You can also choose to enable it for 30 seconds every time you tap the screen when the display is off. Here is how to go about it:

- In the Lock screen settings page, click on "Always On Display".
- Tap Display mode

- Select your desired display mode from the options in the dialogue.

You can customize even further by selecting various clock styles.

- In the Lock screen settings, tap "Clock style"
- Tap "Always On Display"
- Choose your preferred clock face from the options provided.
- Select a color from the Color tab
- Tap "Done" to save the selections

## Flash Notifications

The Samsung Galaxy S20 does not have LED notifications, but there is an option to enable Flash Notification. To do this;

- Go to Settings

- Scroll down and tap Accessibility, then click on Advanced Settings

- Tap on Flash Notification for the following options

  o Camera flash: If this option is enabled, the camera flashes every time you get a message or when someone calls you.

  o Screen flash: The screen flashes every time you get a text message.

# Activate Power Saving Mode

Power-saving mode usually comes in handy whenever your phone's battery reaches the critical level and yet you still need to use it a little longer. To do enable this feature;

- Go to Settings
- Scroll down, then tap Device care, it brings another set of sub-menu option.

Samsung Cloud, Smart Switch

G **Google**
Google settings

**Advanced features**
Bixby Routines, Motions and gestures,
One-handed mode

**Digital Wellbeing and parental controls**
Screen time, App timers, Wind Down

**Device care**
Battery, Storage, Memory, Security

**Apps**
Default apps, Permission manager

- Click on Battery, then tap Power mode.

Power Management

**Power mode**
Optimized

**App power management**
Limit battery usage for apps that you don't use often.

**Wireless PowerShare**

Charging

Fast cable charging

Fast wireless charging

- You are presented with the following options;
  - High performance, optimized, medium power saving, and maximum power saving. To extend your phone's battery life, you can choose between medium and maximum power saving.

< Power mode

Select a mode below for highest display quality
or longer battery life.

○ **High performance**
Higher system speed, maximum screen
brightness and resolution. Uses more battery.

◉ **Optimized**
Get the recommended balance of performance
and battery life.

○ **Medium power saving**
Extend battery life by limiting some functions.

○ **Maximum power saving**
Save as much battery as possible.

- Tap on Medium or Maximum depending on
  your preference.

  o Doing so will open the Medium or
  Maximum power saving mode pop-up
  menu with the options to turn off always
  on display or limit CPU speed. You can
  make necessary adjustments to these
  settings then tap Apply when finished.

## Lock screen and security

## Set a secure screen lock

It is important that you secure your device using a secure screen lock (Pattern, PIN, or Password). This is important to set up and enable biometric locks. To do this:

- Go to Settings, click on Lock screen
- Tap Screen lock type and click on a secure screen lock (Pattern, PIN, or Password).
- Tap on the toggle to enable showing notifications on the lock screen. The available options are:
  - View style: Display notification details or hide them and show only an icon.
  - Hide content: Hide notifications in the Notification panel.
  - Notifications to show: You can make a choice on which notifications to show on the Lock screen.

o Show on Always On Display: Shows notifications on the Always on Display screen.

- Click on Done when finished.

## FaceWidgets

FaceWidgets are shortcuts that give you quick access to useful apps you could control from the lock screen, even if you are using the secure screen lock type. Music player, calculator, alarms, weather etc. are information that can be accessed from the lock screen. To enable FaceWidgets.

- Go to "Settings"
- Click on Lock Screen
- Tap on FaceWidgets
- Enable the items you wish to be on the lock screen

## Clock style

Customize the lock screen clock style.

- Go to settings
- Tap on lock screen,
- Scroll down and tap on clock style
- Tap on lock screen, select your desired style from the types, you can also change the color by tapping on color.
- Click Done when through.

## Find My Mobile

Before you can use the Find My Mobile feature, you must turn it on and customize the options. To access your device remotely, visit findmymobile.samsung.com.

To enable this feature;

- Go to Settings, scroll down and tap on Biometrics and security.

- Scroll down and tap on the toggle to enable Location if it is disabled.

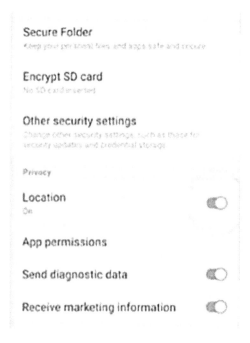

- Scroll up and click on Find My Mobile. If prompted, sign into your Samsung account. Enable the options are available:

o  Remote unlock: Allow Samsung to store
   your PIN, pattern, or password, allowing
   you to unlock and control your device
   remotely.

o  Send last location: Allow your device to send
   its last location to the Find My Mobile server
   when the remaining battery charge falls
   below a certain level.

# Advance Features

In this section, we would be looking at the following features

- Accessories
- Bixby routines
- Smart Capture
- Smart Alert
- Smart Stay
- Dual Messenger
- Double tap to wake up
- Send SOS messages

## Accessories

When you click on the accessories, you get a breakdown of every wired or wireless accessory connected to your smartphone. If they have any specific options it will be displayed.

## Bixby Routines

Bixby routines now these are kind of like a computer program that takes actions when certain conditions are met. You can set certain actions to take place on your phone automatically at certain times. There are several recommended routines, customize each of them and save them into "My routines". so, let's pick this one Before bed routine.

It says if time is equal to and you pick the time that you want so I'm going to pick one time let's just say I go to bed at 12:15 am click done and also you can pick an end time for every routine. Let's just say 9:15 am. So, if time is between 00:15 am. and 9:15 am then turn Bluetooth off. Click "Done" when you are through. This becomes your device's routine when the time is between 00:15am - 9:15am.

## Video Enhancer

With the video enhancer enabled, when you launch any one of the available applications it's going to enhance the video by enhancing the image quality of your videos for you to enjoy brighter and more vivid colors

## Dual Messenger

You can use the Dual Messenger feature to manage two accounts on the Galaxy S20. To do this;

- Open Settings from the home screen.
- Scroll down and Tap Advanced features.
- Tap Dual Messenger.
- Choose the app you want to clone.
- Tap Install on the dialog box to install another instance of the app.
- Tap Confirm to agree to Samsung's terms of use and install the app.

- Enable the Use separate contacts list to Toggle if you want to use a secondary set of contacts with the cloned app.

- Click on Select your second app contacts to choose the contacts.

- Tap Add to add contacts.

- Choose your desired contacts from the list.

- Tap Done to complete the installation.

## Motions and Gestures

Under this menu, we have other options e.g.

### Lift to Wake

Make sure you keep the "Lift to wake" feature enabled. Basically, what it does is that it allows the screen of your device to turn ON when you pick it up.

## Double tap to wake up

This is another option that you should enable in the Galaxy S20. When this feature is enabled, the phone wakes up when the screen is double tapped.

## Smart Stay

This is not a must enabled feature. However, you can choose to keep it ON. So basically, the Smart stay keeps the screen ON while you are looking at it by using the front-camera to detect your face. As long as you are staring at your phone, maybe reading or watching a move it will detect your face and make sure the screen is open.

## Smart Alert

This is a great option. If it is enabled, let's say for example you place your phone on the bed and left to take a shower and while at the bathroom, you have a couple of calls or messages. When you come back and pick up your phone, it is going to vibrate letting you know that there are pending notifications waiting for you to glance at. That vibrational feedback you get when you lift the phone is known as smart alert.

## Easy Mute

When this feature is enabled, there are some things you can do to make the phone mute without even touching it when an alarm goes off or a call comes in. Let say a you don't wish to receive an incoming call; all you need to do is put your hand over the screen and the phone will be muted. The other option with the Easy mute is to flip the phone over with the screen facing down to mute it.

## One-Handed Mode

The Samsung One UI which the GalaxyS20 runs on is designed so you can navigate or control through different apps and settings using just a hand and within reach of your thumb. But there is also a true one-handed mode that you can use. To activate the one-handed mode,

- Go to "Settings"
- Go to the "Advanced features."
- Tap on "Motions and gestures."
- Enable the "One-handed mode."
- When you go inside the "One-handed mode" by clicking on it, you will see that the One-handed mode can be activated in two ways – "Gestures" or "Buttons." To activate it in button mode, tap the Home button three times and the true one-handed mode will be activated. You can justify the screen to the left or right based on which hand you are holding your phone with. Now the entire phone is fully usable with one thumb without having to worry about using your second hand.

## Palm swipe to capture

You can take a screenshot of your phone by simply swiping the edge of your palm across the face of the phone. You do have to touch the actual screen while swiping for this to take effect.

## Swipe to call or send messages

If you are in your "phone application," "contacts" or "recent calls" what you can do is that you can swipe across any of your phone contacts to make a call or send a message. If you swipe to the right, it will call the contact, while if you swipe to the left, it will send a message.

## Samsung Dex Mode Experience

The Samsung Dex experience is a desktop-like experience you get from your Samsung Galaxy S20 series by just plugging it to a monitor or a Television using a USB-C-to-HDMI adaptor. This is one of the best desktop-like experience on a mobile device to date.

The Samsung Dex Experience is nothing new, but in this section, we will be looking at the ONE UI version of Samsung Dex running on the Galaxy S20.

The items for this connection include;

- USB-C-to-HDMI adaptor. This has three USB-A ports one HDMI port and two USB-C ports. The USB-A port allows you to connect a keyboard to your phone. You can also attach a wireless keyboard if you wish to sit back on a couch while using the Samsung Dex.
- Any HDTV or Monitor with HDMI-in (or USB-C in) port

- Your Samsung Galaxy S20 smartphone

Connect the phone to the Monitor or TV, once they are connected, the Samsung Dex is triggered, and it starts on your device and it displays on the Monitor or Tv.

You will get notification on your phone, the notifications are;

1. Mirror your smartphone to the Monitor or TV
2. Is to use your smartphone as a touchpad

You can customize the entire Dex experience from the wallpaper, you can also pin applications to the local taskbar at the bottom of the screen.

The Apps on the Dex experience is a little bit different from the phone Apps. Although the phone apps can be accessed on Dex mode, not all Dex applications can be accessed on your device.

Samsung Dex experience also gives gamers the ability to play mobile games in full screen. However, the controls are different from what you get on your smartphone. You would need to attach a Bluetooth controller to have a better gaming experience on the Samsung Dex.

## Samsung Galaxy S20 Troubleshooting

### How to Factory Reset

A factory reset will delete all the user's personal information including apps, files and settings. You should backup necessary files be before factory reset, as it will be difficult to recover them after the reset.

- Go to Settings
- Scroll down and tap General management.
- Tap Reset, then click on Factory data reset.
- Scroll down to the bottom of the screen and click the Reset button.
- Click on the Delete all button to proceed with the reset.

### Network Connection Errors

Performing this reset has been deemed among the most effective solutions to various types of problems affecting the phone's wireless network services. And here's how it works.

- Go to Settings

- Scroll down and tap General management

- Tap Reset to continue.

- Select Reset network settings from the given options.

- Tap on Reset settings

- Tap Reset to confirm that you'd like to reset the network settings on your Galaxy S20.

The phone will then instigate a network setting reset and then wipes all existing network configurations including customized network options on the phone.

## Accidentally launching apps or edge panels

If you find apps or edge panels opening because of accidental touches, Samsung galaxy S20 includes a feature to prevent these mistakes from being detected.

- Open the Settings app on your device

- Scroll down to Display

- Enable the Accidental touch protection toggle

## Bluetooth devices not connecting properly

If you are having issues with Bluetooth on your Galaxy S20, simply follow these steps to reset your Bluetooth cache, while clearing out any existing devices:

- Go to Settings
- Scroll down to Apps
- Find the Bluetooth app and select it
- Tap Clear Cache

# Books by the Author

Apple Watch Series 5 User's Guide
https://www.amazon.com/dp/B07YD1YLYC